ADAM L.S.

The Scoreboard

First published by Raguel Studios 2024

First edition

Illustration by Karen Keeline

This book was professionally typeset on Reedsy.
Find out more at reedsy.com

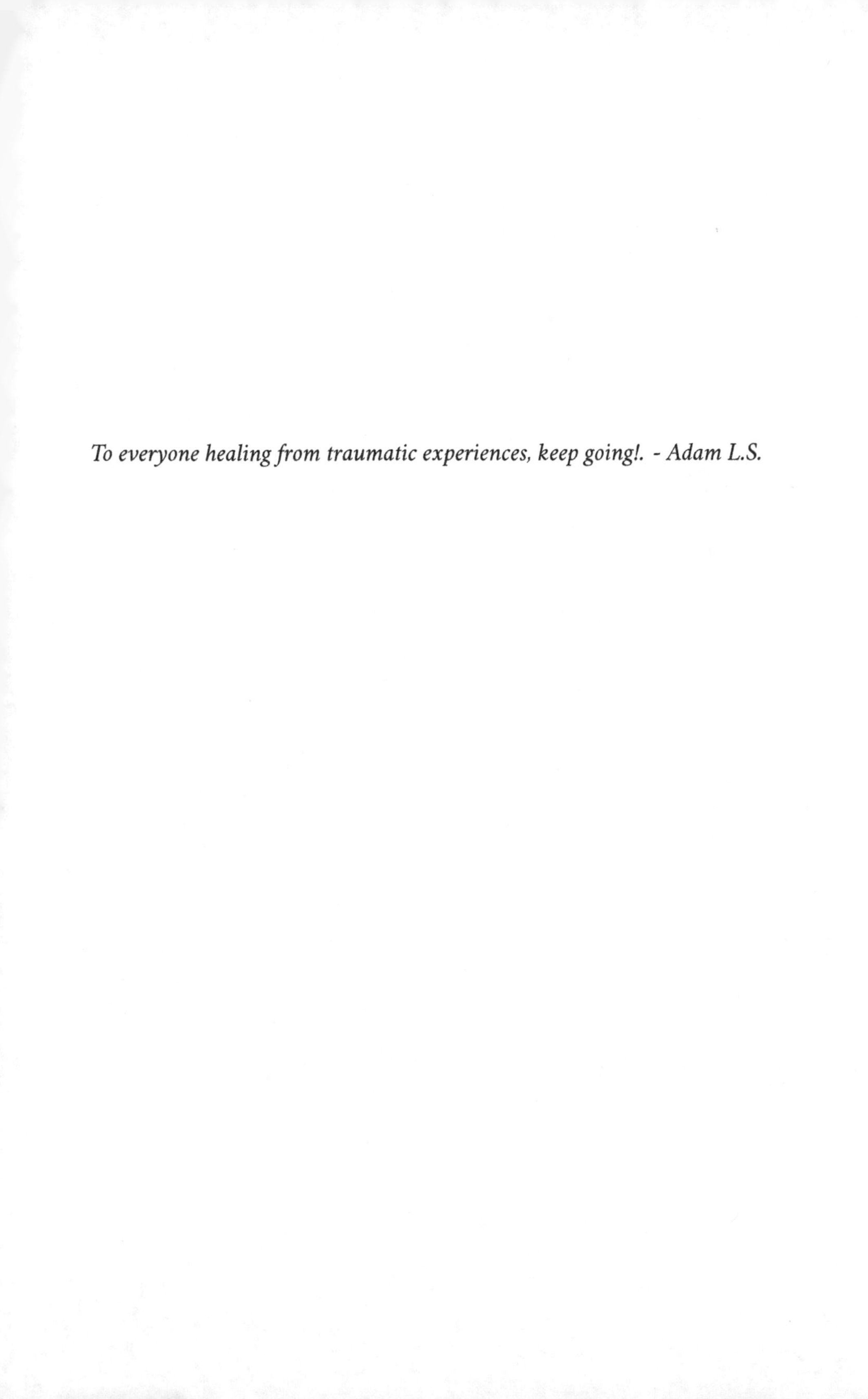

To everyone healing from traumatic experiences, keep going!. - Adam L.S.

You are not alone. - Adam L.S.

Contents

Acknowledgments

To my uncle Karl. - Adam L.S.

I

Chapter 1: Rediscovering

Stops & Starts

Peeking into that deserted valley,
  where there are many stops and starts.
Trauma interrupted the plot,
  they could go on with their lives.

I could not.

Adam L.S.

The Monster

The noise, the fireworks, the heat...
  Would drive him crazy.

He behaved like a monster.
  When agitated, he would storm out.
Offering no relief, he wounded many.
  Everyone tip toed in his presence.

Adam L.S.

Puzzling

I was an outspoken opponent to all,
had outbursts of explosive rage,
a terrifying temper,
filled with anger.

My behavior was puzzling,
it caused war among those closest to me.

I was unable to find any real pleasure, back then.

Adam L.S.

Transformed

I felt frozen and trapped in ice,
  I wanted to escape but did not know how.

Awful memories made it so that I damaged any chemistry set.
  My fear circuits were altered.

Trauma had transformed everything in front of me.

Adam L.S.

PTSD

Wartime trauma,
  the traumatic neuroses of war.

I believed I was a shell shocked solider in the streets.
  Feeling withdrawn and detached life seemed futile.

PTSD.

Adam L.S.

Bearing Witness

I beared witness to pain,
  and lives shattered.

Broken down, over the brink,
  sharing danger, sharing dark secrets.

Would I ever feel alive again?

Adam L.S.

Part Of Me

The memory of what happened,
   and my friends death.

Paralyzed me in shame,
   I went in to a frenzy.

It was impossible for me to ever go home,
   part of me was forever destroyed.

It feels impossible to engage in intimate relationships now.
   I felt brutally violated.

Adam L.S.

I Felt Numb

Bewildered about the differences,
  between love and terror, pain and pleasure.

I felt numb.

I had sought love,
  but my heart was frozen.

So I floated thru space aimlessly.
  I had lost my energy and sense of focus.

Adam L.S.

The Study

Trauma changed my perceptions and imagination,
 it was as though I had enrolled in a nightmare study.

I felt alone, my mind was flooded with unbearable images.
 I could not stop crying. Those images burned in.

Feeling psychotic, triggered, suffering from memories,
 I had been displaced.

I was in psychosis.

Adam L.S.

Ink

A mental image,
like a blot of ink.

I am a meaning making creature.
So as I laid in a meadow, watching the clouds pass me by.

I wondered,
could these clouds, like inkblots,
tell me how my mind worked?

Adam L.S.

Deciphering Reality

I superimpose my trauma on everything and everyone,
  I have trouble deciphering what is real.

I am not mentally flexible,
  I lack the hallmark of imagination,

I wanted to leave the routine of my everyday existence,
  I wanted to envision new possibilities.

I am constantly pulled into the past.

Adam L.S.

So Divided

Those sensations of terror and emptiness,
were so vital to my war.

The trauma made my world so divided,
those that did not walk the same path as I could not be trusted.

I trudged the winter snow storms,
feeling paralyzed, with a dagger plunged through my heart.

I only felt alive when I revisited my past.

When I came back to life,
I began to speak with great intensity.

Adam L.S.

Post Traumatic Stress

I had all sorts of issues,
   substance abuse, depression, mood disorder, schizophrenia.

I tried every treatment, I tried every drug.

I was often inadvertently triggered,
   with a a full blown flashback.

Adam L.S.

Shut Down

Issues I thought I had left behind…
  Family violence, being abused both physically and mentally.

It was so puzzling.
  I had shut down, emotionally.

Adam L.S.

The Source

The source of my terror and pain, were the ones I trusted most.
  The impact of it all was so traumatic.

My body remained hyper vigilant and prepared to be assaulted.
  I had to formulate new avenues of repair.

Adam L.S.

Schizo

I had serious mental problems,
  depression, panic, anxiety and mania.
  Along with symptoms of schizophrenia.
My behavior was irrational, and unpredictable.
  I was frozen in fear.

Adam L.S.

So Much Violence

Assaulted, abandoned and neglected.
  There was so much violence.

In the wake of the trauma I was so self destructive.
  I received electroshock treatment.

Adam L.S.

Bizarre

I had such bizarre and frustrating temper tantrums,
in the face of terrifying and confusing realities.

Was I misunderstood? Or was I wrong?

Adam L.S.

Balance The Boat

I had to shift position,
   I have to balance the boat.

I held that trauma within my body.
   I realized one day, this suffering was related to love and loss.

I was incapable of acknowledging or experiencing the reality of life,
   its pleasures and its heartbreaks.

Adam L.S.

Discrete

Discrete disorders,
  intolerable feelings and relationships.

My behaviors were an adaptation to the complexities of the world.
  A new paradigm was emerging.

Anger, lust, pride, greed, avarice and sloth.

A chemical imbalance,
  was caused by my mental illness.

Adam L.S.

Each November

Suicidally depressed each November,
  losing my patience, and considering visiting an insane asylum.

I felt locked into a life so terrifying,
  a warped reality.

Could I ever experience optimism again?
  Would I conquer this human misery?

Adam L.S.

Cages

Neuron to neuron,
  I had to engage with the rest of the world.

I had so many lingering questions,
  so much traumatic stress.

Like dogs trapped in cages,
  I felt this inescapable shock.

I made no attempt to flee,
  even when the door was wide open,
  I just laid there.

Adam L.S.

Risked It

I wanted to find the road to freedom,
  so I risked experimenting with new options.

I fought, I took action,
  in an attempt to stave off what they said was inevitable.

Long after the danger had passed,
  I found keys to a door leading to a road,
  the road to freedom.

Adam L.S.

Help

Damn this cage!
  I wanted to escape.

Help!
  There was nothing I could do to defend myself.

Teach me how!
  I was immobilized.

Adam L.S.

The Beat Down

Was I addicted to trauma?
   Did I find pleasure in pain?

I felt constant horror and grief.
   Always feeling a vague sense of emptiness.

I felt alive when angry, under duress,
   participating in some dangerous activity.

We beat each other down.

Adam L.S.

Repelled

The memoirs of a brief relationship,
  she was repelled, that damn addict.

I was severely beaten.
  It was a painful situation.

I hated myself,
  I could not stop reliving the trauma from it all.

Adam L.S.

Flames

I was attracted to danger,
  even when I felt immense fear.

I was attracted to the flames that burned us all.
  I was attracted to anyone that would end up hurting me.

Adam L.S.

Why?

I felt so wounded,
could I use these strong emotions to block future pains?

I was traumatized by it all,
but I kept re-exposing myself to stressful situations.
Why did I keep going back?

Adam L.S.

Rejected

A sound, an image, a body sensation…
  I perceived them all as a threat.

My fear system clearly worked.
  I felt devastated by the slightest rejection.

Adam L.S.

Monkey

I could not maintain eye contact.
  I was a low-ranking monkey.

Was I manipulative?
  I would binge, and purge, with everything, with everyone.

I was dramatic.
  I was chronically depressed.

Adam L.S.

Demands

Overwhelmed by demands,
  I mistreated her.

I needed to learn to live in the present,
  instead of being locked in the past.

Adam L.S.

Fifty Fifty

I had less than a fifty fifty chance.
I had lost the motivation to solve my problem.

I stopped asking questions about how she felt, what she thought.
I had lost control of my emotions.

And my emotions controlled my reactions.

Adam L.S.

Get Fixed

Finally, a hint of perspective…
  I had to gain control over my impulses.

I had to become less reactive.
  I no longer wanted to live on an island amongst the midst of misery.

I had to find a safe space,
  a space to get fixed.

Adam L.S.

Sand Castle

My brain disease, had taken control of my fate.

Life had to become more manageable, I had to be less aggressive.
I did not want anything that interfered with my motivation.

I am curious about the world, I want to play in the sand.
Building a sand castle was imperative for maturing.

Creating that sand castle made me a well functioning, contributing member of society.

Adam L.S.

Equilibirum

I no longer wanted to use drugs.

There had to be other means of changing my physiology and inner equilibrium.

Adam L.S.

Four Truths

I heard of the four fundamental truths…

1. Our capacity to destroy is matched by our capacity to heal.
2. Language gives us the power to heal.
3. We have the ability to regulate our physiology.
4. We can change our social environments.

Adam L.S.

Activity

I gazed into the fantastic darkness...
   The hemisphere divided, I had lived in that dark space.

There were undreamed of capacities for understanding why it all happened.
   I had to process the information I had.

I began to map out the circuits of my mind and consciousness,
   this fueled my neural activity.

Adam L.S.

Hijacked

Like trying to understand a cars engine,
neuro-imaging made it possible to see inside.

I studied what happened to my mind during that period.
It had been hijacked.

Images, feelings and sounds, lingered on.
I collected those fragments.

I kept the ones where I felt safe and in control.
Those fragments were worth saving.

Adam L.S.

Mothers Arms

I laid in my mothers arms,
as she cried.

She could not free herself.
Her heart pounded I trembled.

I listened to her breathing.
She was filled with self blame.

Adam L.S.

Jump

My children were intolerable,
  their laughter became a powerful trigger.

My heart would race,
  My blood pressure would jump.

Adam L.S.

She Tried

I looked defeated, I froze.
  My breathing was shallow, my eyes wide, shoulders hunched.

She tried to comfort me,
  there would be a price for her distress.

Adam L.S.

The King

It was a speechless horror…
   My color had changed.
   My blood supply was diminishing.

A flashback had been triggered.
   A flashback of a murdered king.

Adam L.S.

The Edge

It was a horrible masterpiece.
All the victims…

Assaulted.

Trauma by nature drove me to the edge,
the edge of comprehension.

Adam L.S.

Just Words

Words failed,
  haunting images captured the experiences,
  to return as nightmares and flashbacks.

Adam L.S.

Unmodified

Fragments of trauma,
sounds, smells, and physical sensations.

All of it, triggered flashbacks that brought me back into consciousness,
unmodified by the passage of time.

Adam L.S.

Scan

The scans revealed it on my right side,
  my left. On the top and the bottom.

Adam L.S.

Vocab

The vocabulary all of those events…

I could not sequence them I could not identify the effect.
The effects were long term. Why did I act that way?

I had to create coherent plans for my future.

Adam L.S.

Adrenaline

My heart rate increased, the readings for my blood pressure spiked.
It reflected my frantic state, like an alarm.

Adrenaline coursed through me,
it was critical to help me fight back or flee
in the face of danger.

Adam L.S.

Down

Responses became muted…
  That was then, this is now.

The method of how to talk about my distressing feelings was lost.
  My rational brain desired resolve.

I'm continually impressed about how it all went down.
  So I wrote my story, of victimization and revenge.

Adam L.S.

Before Us

I ran for my life,
  I could not see color, nor hear sound in the universe.
  I lacked feeling, or emotion.

Before us, the universe was also free of pain and anxiety.

Adam L.S.

The Clock

I ran through the rubble, ash and smoke that morning.
  I made my way among the rescue crews.

I watched the blazing lights around the clock.
  I jumped from the towers windows into that black circle.

Adam L.S.

Trampoline

Like a trampoline,
  I was a witness to it all. The unspeakable mayhem and disaster.

So I made a drawing.
  Using my imagination I began to go on with my life.

I had grown up.

Adam L.S.

Caregivers

I could not grasp that tragedy,
  they were my caregivers. They left psychological scars.

My brain, and my body could not be quieted.

Adam L.S.

Entirety

To imagine a creative alternative...
  other than remaining stopped in my growth.

I had to integrate new experiences.
  A threw out that sad memento.

I enrolled in trauma treatment to engage.
  I engaged my entire organism, mind and body, to safety.

Adam L.S.

Alarm System

My whole body responded to threats,
my brains alarm system sounded. I had pre-programmed escape plans.

The old brain would take over however,
I wanted to use the higher brain, my conscious mind.

Adam L.S.

Effective Action

Fight/flight/freeze...
  I could not regain my senses this time.

A war zone, an accident...
  I needed to take effective action.

I had to learn to escape a threat that no longer existed.

Adam L.S.

Move

Move, do something!
  It was a critical factor, learning to protect myself.

I had to help myself,
  to survive, to flourish.

Adam L.S.

Secondary

Everything else is secondary,
  I began listening to internal signals.

Food, rest, protection, shelter,
  a map of the world was right there.

Adam L.S.

Sustaining

Just sustaining life…
I sought internal balance, homeostasis.

So I began to consider the complexities of my life, mind and behaviors.
I was told this is a common case for traumatized children and adults.

For survival purposes.

Adam L.S.

Always Moving

The world is always moving…

So I set out to discover what happens when I cried, smiled or protested.

Adam L.S.

In Tune

I wanted to understanding abstract, symbolic ideas.
I planned for tomorrow, I wanted to be in tune.

Adam L.S.

Abstract

Within the animal kingdom,
  there is abstract thought.

As well as excitement and linguistic feats.
  Plan, reflect, neglect, save.

Adam L.S.

Mirroring

Mirroring each trauma,
  resulted in sensational empathy and discoveries.

My language was developing.

Adam L.S.

Each Other

Our voices take on the same rhythms,
  and they are vulnerable to each other.

Invariably, this involves not feeling seen.
  I resisted being hijacked by negativity.

Adam L.S.

Off Line

Through out our entire lifespan,
  we have a major impact.

We have to filter out irrelevant information from out exposure to trauma however,
  do we still remain vulnerable to going off line in response to threats?

Adam L.S.

Edge of Impulse

Discovery and wonder…

Who rouses our desires? Why do we blow up?

On the edge of impulse and acceptable behavior,
are where most of our troubles begin.

Adam L.S.

Dibs

Emotional first dibs, on new information...
About the environment and body state...

What I witnessed, heard, felt, processed at lightning speed.
Could take the high road?

My go to responses, prolonged startle and aggressive outbursts.
I was aware of the danger but did not realize what was happening...
Before it was to late.

My body became triggered.
I was unable to recover.

Adam L.S.

Faulty Alarm

In danger or safe?
  Never. Always. Who knew?
  Painful understandings.

I had a faulty alarm system.
  I'd blow up or shut down.

Adam L.S.

I'm Smiling

I had to abort this stress response.
  I learned to meditate.

Hovering calmly and objectively over my thoughts, feelings and emotions.
  They call it, mindfulness? Being mindful?

Whatever it's called, I'm smiling again.

Adam L.S.

Watchtower

My watchtower…
  My breathing, movement, and touch.
  I had to upgrade the threat detection system.

Meditation and yoga helped.

Adam L.S.

Unruly

The foundation, my experiences…
  I needed to find balance so it would not collapse or crumble.

I had unruly horses,
  As the rider, I was unruly.

Adam L.S.

The Bell

The alarm bell rang,
  signaling my emotional brain.
  I was in danger.

Would no amount of insight silence it?
  It reminded me of a comedy.

Adam L.S.

Sitting

The techniques are terrific,
  I am not angry anymore.

I sit with someone I love and can depend on.
  Alone, with them, with him or her.

Anywhere.
  Everywhere.

Adam L.S.

Tug-o-War

I loved tug of war. Most of the time.

In the theater of,
   physical discomfort and psychological misery, I did not.

I just wanted to win the key of understanding.

Adam L.S.

Halfway

Halfway through the journey,
  I started running.

Through the dense fog, a visibility of zero.

In a split second I could slam into a wall,
  and be at sideways standstill.

I would never again be responsible for a pile up,
  of some of the worst disasters in history.

Adam L.S.

Screaming

I screamed, "get me out of here!"
  I would not leave unscathed.

Adam L.S.

The Question

That night…
  I had to let go, or I would die.

The images,
  So haunting.

The questions,
  went on and on.

What if I had left sooner?

Adam L.S.

Loop

I was trapped,
  sweating, in a perpetual loop of a flashback.

My blood pressure stayed sky high.

Adam L.S.

All The Time

The flashbacks got worse, ya know?
  They happen, all the time.

Like drowning in a pool.

Adam L.S.

Weary

I was asleep, and unsure of how long it would last.
  I was compulsively numb.
  I was in a dangerous situation.
  I was fatigued, depressed, and weary.

Adam L.S.

War Zone

The deep memories,
  made it impossible to feel alive.

Imprisoned in the past.
  The war zone.

Adam L.S.

Imprints

Natural pleasures caused me to have a migraine,
I viewed everyone as a monster.

Were all our origins traumatic?
Was my threat perception system damaged?

I live with the imprints of my past.

Adam L.S.

Mastery

Terrible things happen,
 I would gain mastery over my internal sensations and emotions.

Adam L.S.

Smoking

The crash activated, triggered a powerful stress.
My heart raced.

Smashed, smoking, a raging fire…

My amygdala went into overdrive.

I was chronically scared that people hated me,
and were out to get me.

Adam L.S.

The Timekeeper

The timekeeper collapsed.
  Deactivated.

I was trapped in that moment.

Whatever is happening is finite.
  It will come to an end, sooner or later.

Adam L.S.

Pulled

That wretched state,
   I thought I'd never get over that loss.
   I thought, "this will last forever."

Always re-registering.
   made it so I was never fully online.

I wanted to feel calm, safe and grounded.
   I'm done being pulled into the past.

Adam. L.S.

Hyperfocus

The flashbacks evoked a sense of…
  Terror and helplessness.

This created a gnawing in my stomach.
  This created tunnel vision and hyper focus.

Adam. L.S.

Shut Down

The price of shutting down pleasure and joy,
was numbness and a blank mind.

Adam. L.S.

Blank Stares

Depersonalized…
  Blank stares, absent mindedness.
  Massive dissociation.

I thwarted the next flashback,
  to escape that crash.

My emotions no longer roared.

Adam. L.S.

Valiant Effort

My energy was drained,
  with each horrendous story.

I did not want to be a lifeless patient,
  I made a valiant effort in prayer for that hour to be over quickly.

Adam. L.S.

Let's Talk

Talk therapy?

I felt trapped, demolished,
  I was in survival mode.

I wanted to make myself disappear.

Adam. L.S.

Bit by Bit

I acted out to get attention,
 I didn't mean to mean to bother anybody.
 However, I lost my future bit by bit.

Adam. L.S.

Took a Walk

My PTSD dominated me,
  it was difficult to feel fully alive.

Every where I went I was filled with horror and misery.
  I had to learn to reduce my emotional outbursts.

So many misunderstandings.
  I took a walk.

I wouldn't let life pass me by.

Adam. L.S.

Machine

My body-brain connection intensified,
  My heart pumped, I vibrated, I am a rhythm machine.

Adam. L.S.

The Intro

The emotions of man and animals…
  The origins of our species…
  The foundation…

This is a terrific introduction.

Adam. L.S.

Vestiges

I observed gratitude and magnanimous all around me…

However my animalistic emotions were always present,
  the hairs on the back of my neck stood up when frightened.
  I'd grit and bare my teeth when enraged.

These were the vestiges of a long evolutionary process.

Adam. L.S.

Back Off

I'd snarl at random,
  my lip and tooth raised at whomever I addressed.

My threatening posture, cautioning them.
  Back off.

Adam. L.S.

Signaled

My sadness attracted care and attention,
  my fears signaled my helplessness.

Adam. L.S.

The Dynamics

I'd try to read the dynamics of people…

Were they tense or relaxed?
  What did their posture or tone of voice mean?

Their facial expressions.
  It was a beautiful foreign language.

Adam. L.S.

I Evolved

I evolved.

I no longer tried to escape,
  or exhibited avoidance behaviors.

I became part of that successful species.

Adam. L.S.

Reciprocals

There were reciprocals of avoidance and escape,
  stuck in survival mode,
  fighting unseen enemies,
  with no room for nurture care or love.

Adam. L.S.

Invisible Assaults

Against invisible assaults my closest bonds were threatened.

To win, I had to imagine, plan, play, learn and pay attention,
  to other people's needs.

I had to listen to my heart and mind,
  I had to communicate on an intimate level.

Adam. L.S.

Clung

My excitement grew…
  And I was devastated.

I had clung desperately, to another.

Adam. L.S.

Inner Landscape

Replace overwhelming emotions with definable sensations...

I found ways to help people,
  I altered my inner sensory landscape.

This is a traditional healing practice,
  all over the world.

Adam. L.S.

New Me

I had to transform my understanding of trauma and recovery, this is a valiant purpose. I like this new me.

Adam. L.S.

CBT

The bell rang,
  it was time to fill my plate.

The association between bell and food is known as extinction.
  This is CBT.

Adam. L.S.

Laid There

Unscathed?
  Physically.

Broke down.
  Emotionally. Behaviorally. Physiologically.

I laid there motionless.

Adam. L.S.

Obliterated

Ongoing terror!
  The signs were there.

I felt obliterated!
  I was no longer curious.

Adam. L.S.

Equilibrium

It was a full blown startle reaction.
  I acted as though I was trapped in a cage.

My equilibrium broke down.

Adam. L.S.

Dog

This inescapable shock…
  My entire organism could not do a thing.
  It was inevitable.

This phenomenon…
  My learned helplessness.
  I felt humiliated, the agony of a rabid dog in a cage.

Adam. L.S.

Maintain

I wanted to maintain this,
  this loving relationship.

I wanted to escape my hurt, pain and betrayal.
  This was the ultraparadoxical stage.

Adam L.S.

Reflex

My positivity responses to negative stimuli,
  kept me in a perpetual loop.

Did this reflex have a purpose?
  All creatures need a purpose.

Adam. L.S.

Appetite

To make my way in the world,
  my purpose required movement and emotions.

My emotions propelled me to act.
  Food, sex, combat…

I had an appetite.

Adam. L.S.

Nervous System

I peered into the window of the nervous system,
all the little signs, the muscle glitches.

The other persons eye movements.
Their speed of voice.

I wanted to be a product of synchrony.

Adam. L.S.

Time To Heal

The body's accelerator, sympathy.
  The brake, parasympathetic.

These manage the body's energy flow
  These prepare us for its conversations.

Would there be fight or flight?
  I needed to heal either way.

Adam. L.S.

Sped Up

My heart sped up.
  I always chose to fight,
  until that day.

I stopped moving thru time.
  I just laid there.

Adam L.S.

Hyperdrive

As I breathed my heart would either speed up, or slow down.
Even during yoga and meditation.

It has not slowed down since last winter.

Adam. L.S.

Love Code

My neural love code…
Told me when I was safe, or when I was in danger.
The interplay was subtle.

Rage came,
mental collapse followed.

I never felt calm again.

Adam L.S.

My Tribe

All of my relationships have been satisfying or difficult…
Focus, discover, treat…

I want to be part of my tribe.

Adam. L.S.

Our Species

Small acts of kindness, connection…
  Benevolence should triumph over malevolence.

The core of our species…
  I feel safe with other people, now.

Adam L.S.

Prescriptions

My mental health was a smoke screen.
  Why do they seem so satisfied with their life?
  I wanted to be truly heard and seen.
  Could I exist in someone elses mind and heart?

They prescribed me friendship and love.

Adam. L.S.

People Peopling

Well functioning?
  Pffffffft…

That's all it takes?

To acknowledge the humanity of others?

Wow…

Adam. L.S.

You're Going To Be Ok

So many levels of safety…

I had to reset my physiology.
I had to make it so my survival mechanisms weren't working against me.
I had to recover the capacity to relax and experience true reciprocity.

I wanted to engage , I wanted to be social. I wanted to feel safe.

Adam. L.S.

Signals

I had not activated the smile muscle in some time.
  My voice box did not create laughter.

My heart received signals today,
  I did both.

I activated my social engagement system.
  I could breathe again.

Adam. L.S.

Changed

My tone changed.
  My face changed.

I spoke faster.
  My heart beat faster.

There was no way out.
  There was the ultimate emergency system.

Adam. L.S.

Fright

This immobilization…
  This panic…
  This rage…

To survive the trauma,
  and be so frightened and frightening.

Adam. L.S.

So Complex

I went numb,
  the situation was so complex.

Running did not take care of the threat.
  This is my last resort.

Adam. L.S.

It Was

I fostered a deep sense of pleasure and connection,
  That scream was strong enough to penetrate the root.

My heart and breathing slowed.
  I felt my surroundings dings, was this real?

Adam. L.S.

Why?

My natural state, was "on guard",
  I showed vigilance, I kept trying.

Adam. L.S.

Landmarks

The landmark,
  my earliest memories of abuse and neglect.

They knew I'd be a victim of violence.
  Physical contact triggered intense reactions.

Adam. L.S.

Smile

Chronic shut down,
angry, frozen.

That waiting period, alone in that room.
I flashed her a big smile when we met again.

Adam. L.S.

Simple…

It's simple,
  when I allow my movements to be rhythmically attuned.

Adam. L.S.

Bypassed

I bypassed my mind,
  I engaged my safety system.
  I sat so still, so alone, so peaceful.

Adam. L.S.

Joyful Patterns

They promote new physical education,
  providing joyful engagement.

I was no longer enraged.
  Therapeutic yoga, on repeat, my new pattern.

Adam. L.S.

Shift Gears

My body kept the score.
  Those heartbreaking, gut wrenching emotions.

It called for a radical shift.

Adam. L.S.

Unsolved

I lost myself,
  my body,
  my damn mind.

I tried to be patient and love the questions.
  The riddles remain unsolved.

Adam. L.S.

Pretender

She pretended to joke,
  but her words, what she said, she was serious.

Adam. L.S.

Where To?

Do physical abuse victims have anywhere to turn?
Or are they always trying to find their place?

Adam. L.S.

Shelter

I was curled up, terrified…
  All the time.

I was in a violence shelter.

Adam. L.S.

I Wasn't Ready Yet

I cried while trying to take care of myself.
 I couldn't take care of her.

Adam. L.S.

Wtf

She moved…
 I said, "where are you? "

I felt extremely disconnected.
 That was a traumatic neglect.

Adam. L.S.

Under Her Spell

Losing her control.
I was amazed.
I could not even begin to guess what she was.

Adam. L.S.

Just Stop, Please

How do we know we are alive?
  We survived the trauma, didn't we?
  When do we stop thinking of the past?

Adam. L.S.

Idled POS

My brain idled.
  I was unaware I could be self aware.
  I was not awake.

My brain kept on churning.

Adam. L.S.

Myself

My sense of self,
  was my brightest, largest region of my mind.

My internal GPS.
  My watchtower.

It was destroyed that day.

Adam. L.S.

Mohawk

A Mohawk of self awareness...

Each side a contrast,
  scans of an orientation in space...

On my time here,
  of my trauma.

Adam. L.S.

Transmit

Dread persisted long after,
  I went to shut down the transmit of those visceral feelings and emotions.

Those signals defined my terror.

Adam. L.S.

Efficiency

My physical sensations…
  A piece of music…
  A siren…
  A shift in temperature…
  A hunger for sex…

Everything going on within.
  The electrical messages sent to my nerves.

I became astoundingly efficient in regulating my breathing.

Adam. L.S.

Who Told You?

The wordless knowledge ever present,
  I had to maintain balance without data.

Adam L.S.

The End.

The threat was there,
  our love would be annihilated.

My sleep was disturbed,
  my heart sank.

Adam L.S.

Also by Adam L.S.

The Forest is poetry exploring suffering and the cause of suffering; delving into prayer, mediation, and fasting; the basic truths of life; traditional styles of mentoring and how we become manifestations of compassion.

The Forest
Coming soon!

www.ingramcontent.com/pod-product-compliance
Lightning Source LLC
LaVergne TN
LVHW012058160826
845678LV00014B/2874
9798227025333